Data Protection and the Cloud

Are the risks too great?

Data Protection and the Cloud

Are the risks too great?

PAUL TICHER

IT Governance Publishing

IT Governance Publishing
IT Governance Limited
Unit 3, Clive Court
Bartholomew's Walk
Cambridgeshire Business Park
Ely, Cambridgeshire
CB7 4EA
United Kingdom

www.itgovernance.co.uk

© Paul Ticher 2015

First published in the United Kingdom in 2015
by IT Governance Publishing.

ISBN 978-1-84928-712-8

PREFACE

One of the most dramatic recent developments in computing has been the rapid take-up of cloud applications. There is no sign of this diminishing, with the increasing proliferation of small, mobile devices which presuppose always-on internet connections and rely heavily on the cloud.

The business advantages of the cloud are clear, both for the provider and the user. The provider can move to a subscription model for small users as well as large. The user gets the flexibility of being able to access both data and applications from any location, avoids much of the burden of applying security or productivity upgrades to their software and has the option of multi-platform access to an integrated set of data.

Cloud usage is continuing to expand. It is suggested1, for example, that the market has grown at least three-fold between 2008 and 2014, and that over 86% of businesses are already using some type of cloud computing. This is no longer just a toe in the water. Highly confidential and business-critical data is routinely placed in the cloud. There are predictions that over 50% of all information technology will be in the cloud within ten years.

Since May 2013, central government departments have been subject to a 'cloud first' policy that requires them to consider cloud-based IT solutions before other options. These departments can only deviate from using cloud-based IT solutions when they can show that alternative offerings provide better value for money than products and services available through the central platform.

The range of applications provided in the cloud is still growing. Data exchange, collaboration tools and backup have now been joined by services that provide the full range of desktop packages, including databases, word processing and

---

[1] Figures are being constantly produced. Any references given here would be quickly out of date.

spreadsheets, by communication tools for bulk email, surveys, event bookings and the like, and of course by social media.

As with all technologies, the legal and practical implications are not always immediately apparent, and unexpected problems can be thrown up. Cloud computing does not sit easily with our current data protection law – hardly surprising when we consider that the World Wide Web itself was in its infancy when EU Directive 95/46/EC was agreed in 1995. The UK's Data Protection Act 1998 is based directly on 95/46/EC.

The consequences of a data protection failure can be considerable. Firstly, of course, to the individuals affected: cases have occurred, thankfully rarely, where serious physical harm has been directly caused through a failure to prevent data falling into the wrong hands, while other damage, including financial, is more common. For the organisation responsible, the consequences include not just enforcement action – including financial penalties – but also the loss of reputation and the impact on brand integrity and customer loyalty that follow from the publicity given to serious breaches.

The ease with which data can be moved around the Web and the user's day-to-day (in fact second-to-second) reliance on the performance of cloud providers, does make data protection compliance more challenging than it might be when data is sitting firmly under control on an in-house server.

Some of the challenges may be addressed if, and when, the EU has completed its overhaul of its data protection regime. At the time of writing it is not clear when this will be concluded, or how much of the current draft will make it through to the final version. The proposed changes are discussed in Chapter 9, but it is unlikely that they will remove the risks inherent in the fundamental nature of cloud computing.

If these risks are managed properly they need not be show-stoppers. The benefits of cloud computing are certainly tempting. The important thing is to be fully aware of the risks and to take appropriate action before deciding to put valuable, confidential data into the cloud.

ABOUT THE AUTHOR

With a background in IT, focused on CRM and other information management applications, Paul has worked on data protection for over 20 years. He is now a well-known consultant on the topic, mainly to non-profit organisations, and specialises in work with charities and voluntary organisations.

Paul is the author of the standard work *Data Protection for Voluntary Organisations* (now in its third edition) as well as materials for ITGP and other publishers. He also carries out data protection reviews and delivers training and webinars on the topic.

ACKNOWLEDGEMENTS

I would like to thank Chris Evans, ITSM Specialist; Christopher Wright, Wright-CandA Consulting Ltd; author of *Agile Governance and Audit*, and ir. H.L. (Maarten) Souw RE, Enterprise Risk and QA Manager, UWV, for their helpful comments during the review process.

x

CONTENTS

Introduction 1
Chapter 1: Background – The Data Protection Principles.. 3
Data protection principles 3
Chapter 2: The Data Controller/Data Processor
Relationship... 9
Data Controller/Data Processor contracts 11
Chapter 3: Security (Seventh Data Protection Principle).. 15
Confidentiality, integrity and availability 15
Data in transit and at rest 16
Security in the cloud 17
Chapter 4: Mitigating Security Risks in the Cloud 21
Cyber Essentials 23
Access controls 24
Other guidance and recommendations 26
Chapter 5: Transfers Abroad (Eighth Data Protection
Principle) 35
Safe Harbor... 37
Chapter 6: Other Data Protection Principles 41
First Data Protection Principle (Fairness, Transparency and
Choice) 41
Second Data Protection Principle (Specified and limited
purposes)... 42
Third Data Protection Principle (Adequate, Relevant and not
Excessive)... 42
Fourth Data Protection Principle (Accuracy)...................... 42
Fifth Data Protection Principle (Limited retention) 43
Sixth Data Protection Principle (Data Subject rights)......... 44
Chapter 7: Other legal and technical implications for cloud
contracts 45
Overriding jurisdictions.. 47
Responding to breaches 47
Chapter 8: Enforcement.. 49
Chapter 9: The proposed new EU Regulation and other
measures 51
Chapter 10: Checklist.. 55
References 57

INTRODUCTION

This book is intended to be an introduction to the risks involved in cloud sourcing, and to enable managers to ask the right questions. Suggestions are offered for the kind of risks an organisation's use of the cloud might generate, and the kind of remedial measures that might be taken. These are given as examples only and are not intended to be a substitute for qualified legal or technical advice. Other publications from ITGP, listed at the end of this book, address security in more detail.

Cloud security has to be a joint effort between the provider and the customer. The customer must select a provider with adequate security and other provisions; many of the topics discussed here will therefore be of equal interest to cloud providers. However, the customer's responsibilities go further. Without a well-functioning information security process in place, selection of a secure cloud provider is only a half-measure.

In order to emphasise where the responsibility for data protection compliance normally lies, the customer for cloud services is more-or-less interchangeably referred to in this publication as the Data Controller.

The Data Protection Act 1998 is generally referred to as 'the Act' in this publication.

This is a UK-focused title, based on UK legislation and experience, and will therefore be of relevance to any organisations that need to operate under the UK Data Protection Act.

Since the web addresses of individual documents can change, references are generally given to the parent website, with suggestions on how to locate the specific document.

CHAPTER 1: BACKGROUND – THE DATA PROTECTION PRINCIPLES

As most readers probably know, the Data Protection Act is based on eight legally-binding principles. Being principles rather than precise stipulations, these describe the outcome that must be achieved, not the means of doing so. Every organisation has a significant degree of flexibility in deciding how to comply.

The Act applies to the whole lifecycle of information, from its original collection to its final destruction. See the definition of 'processing' below.

It is usually necessary to be able to demonstrate, through policies and procedures, staff training and other measures, how an organisation ensures that all of its actions comply with the principles. A failure to comply with the principles is a breach of the Act. Any harm suffered by individuals as a result of a breach could lead to a claim for compensation and the Information Commissioner has powers to impose a financial penalty of up to £500,000 or to take other enforcement action in respect of serious breaches of the Act.

Familiarity with the principles is therefore an essential element in assessing the risks that might be posed by the use of cloud services and the mitigating actions that might be necessary.

Data protection principles

These are quoted from the Data Protection Act 1998, Schedule 1, Part I.

1. Personal data shall be processed fairly and lawfully and, in particular, shall not be processed unless –

   a) at least one of the conditions in Schedule 2 *[see below]* is met

      and

3

(b) in the case of sensitive personal data, at least one of the conditions in Schedule 3 is also met. *[Schedule 3, as subsequently amended by Statutory Instrument, contains around 20 conditions, more restrictive than those in Schedule 2. For the purposes of this publication it is sufficient to assume that particularly great care should be taken with records that include 'sensitive personal data' – defined below.]*

2. Personal data shall be obtained only for one or more specified and lawful purposes, and shall not be further processed in any manner incompatible with that purpose or those purposes.
3. Personal data shall be adequate, relevant and not excessive in relation to the purpose or purposes for which they are processed.
4. Personal data shall be accurate and, where necessary, kept up to date.
5. Personal data processed for any purpose or purposes shall not be kept for longer than is necessary for that purpose or those purposes.
6. Personal data shall be processed in accordance with the rights of data subjects under this Act.
7. Appropriate technical and organisational measures shall be taken against unauthorised or unlawful processing of personal data and against accidental loss or destruction of, or damage to, personal data.
8. Personal data shall not be transferred to a country or territory outside the European Economic Area unless that country or territory ensures an adequate level of protection for the rights and freedoms of data subjects in relation to the processing of personal data.

Implications of the data protection principles for cloud computing

All the data protection principles are aimed firstly at preventing harm to individuals, and secondly at ensuring that they are treated fairly whenever their data is used.

Two of the principles are particularly relevant to cloud computing:

- Principle 7, which says you must have appropriate security, and
- Principle 8, which controls the transfer of data abroad.

Subsequent chapters look at all of the principles in the context of cloud computing. The table below indicates their relative risk profile in relation to cloud computing. This does not imply that these risks would have the same ranking in other contexts. Principles 7 and 8 are considered first and in detail; the remaining principles are discussed in *Chapter 6*.

Principle	*Risk rank*	*Comment*
1. Fairness 2. Limited purposes	Low (Medium)	No different from in-house considerations unless cloud provider also captures personal data for own purposes
3. Adequacy 4. Accuracy	Medium	Minor implications if the design of the cloud application does not support good data quality
5. Retention	Low	No different from in-house considerations
6. Data subject rights	Medium	Possible minor implications for subject access
7. Security	Very high	Significant additional risks from cloud computing
8. Transfers abroad	High	Cloud applications may (without making this obvious) locate data outside 'safe' jurisdictions

Other relevant definitions

This publication is not a treatise on the Act as a whole. It may, however, be useful to clarify a few other relevant definitions from the Act.

Processing: This is defined very broadly, to include effectively any activity involving personal data. The Act defines processing as 'obtaining, recording or holding' the data, or 'carrying out any operation [on it]' including (but not limited to) 'organisation', 'alteration', 'retrieval', 'consultation', 'use', 'disclosure', 'erasure' and 'destruction'. It is hard to see how a cloud application could operate without 'processing' data within the terms of the Act.

Personal data: Information in electronic form that relates in some way to a living individual who can be identified from the data (plus, if relevant, any other available information), falls clearly within the definition of personal data. Non-electronic data is obviously outside the scope of this publication.

Data subject: The individual about whom personal data is held, wherever they are located.

Sensitive personal data: Information about an individual's racial or ethnic origin, political beliefs, religious beliefs, trade union membership, mental or physical health, sex life (including sexuality), offences, alleged offences and court appearances. This information requires special treatment – and often consent for its use. In terms of cloud computing, the loss or compromise of sensitive personal data would be a very serious matter.

Schedule 2 Conditions (at least one of which must be met)

1. *The data subject has given his consent to the processing.*

2. *The processing is necessary –*

   (a) *for the performance of a contract to which the data subject is a party, or*
   (b) *for the taking of steps at the request of the data subject with a view to entering into a contract.*

3. *The processing is necessary for compliance with any legal obligation to which the data controller is subject, other than an obligation imposed by contract.*

4. *The processing is necessary in order to protect the vital interests of the data subject.*

5. *The processing is necessary –*

   (a) *for the administration of justice,*
   (b) *for the exercise of any functions conferred on any person by or under any enactment,*
   (c) *for the exercise of any functions of the Crown, a Minister of the Crown or a government department, or*
   (d) *for the exercise of any other functions of a public nature exercised in the public interest by any person.*

6. *(1) The processing is necessary for the purposes of legitimate interests pursued by the data controller or by the third party or parties to whom the data are disclosed, except where the processing is unwarranted in any particular case by reason of prejudice to the rights and freedoms or legitimate interests of the data subject.*

   (2) The Secretary of State may by order specify particular circumstances in which this condition is, or is not, to be taken to be satisfied.

CHAPTER 2: THE DATA CONTROLLER/DATA PROCESSOR RELATIONSHIP

Responsibility for compliance with the data protection principles and other aspects of the Act lies with the 'Data Controller'.

The **Data Controller** is defined in the Act as "a person who (either alone or jointly or in common with other persons) determines the purposes for which and the manner in which any personal data are ... processed". 'Person' in this context very rarely means an individual (or 'natural person'). Instead, in most cases the Data Controller will be an organisation, although individuals who are in business on their own account can also be Data Controllers. It is important to note that group-level responsibility for data protection compliance is not an option. Each legal entity – company, public body, institution, partnership, or even an unincorporated charity – carries its own separate responsibility.

The cloud provider in many cases will be a **Data Processor**. A Data Processor is defined as "any person (other than an employee of the Data Controller) who processes the data on behalf of the Data Controller". Bear in mind the definition of 'processing' discussed above, and it will be clear that almost every cloud provider could indeed be processing personal data in some way or another on behalf of the customer, and would therefore be a Data Processor.

Guidance[2] issued by the Information Commissioner in May 2014, however, suggests that in some cases the cloud provider might exercise sufficient control over the 'manner' in which data is processed to become a Data Controller in its own right, and may even determine to some extent the 'purposes'. One example in the guidance is where the cloud provider is processing payments on behalf of an online retailer. The Information Commissioner finds that in the example given, the payment company is a Data Controller because it (quoting from the guidance):

- "decides which information it needs from customers in order to process their payments correctly;
- exercises control over the other purposes the customer's data is used for, for example direct marketing;
- has legal requirements of its own to meet, for example relating to the use and retention of payment card data; and
- has its own terms and conditions that apply directly to the retailer's customers."

Although it would ultimately be for the courts to determine whether a cloud provider was a Data Controller or a Data Processor, it is always useful to establish a common view between the customer and the cloud provider on what the relationship appears to be, as a basis for clarifying their respective responsibilities.

Where a Data Controller employs the services of a Data Processor, full responsibility for data protection compliance remains with the Data Controller. If data is lost in the cloud, or if security is breached, the Data Controller is responsible for any harm caused to the individuals whose data it caused to be placed in the cloud, and could be the subject of enforcement action taken by the Information Commissioner.

---

[2] *Data controllers and data processors: what the difference is and what the governance implications are*, available on the Information Commissioner's website.

Data Controller/Data Processor contracts

The Act is quite specific in its approach to the relationship between the organisation that carries the responsibility – the Data Controller – and any organisation to which work is outsourced – the Data Processor.

The Act requires there to be a contract, 'evidenced in writing', between the Data Controller and the Data Processor, setting out the relationship and imposing security obligations on the Data Processor. The Data Controller is also given a specific responsibility to assess the adequacy of the Data Processor's security, and take steps to verify it.

If there is any possibility, therefore, that the cloud provider is a Data Processor, it would be very unwise for the customer to proceed without a written contract that meets at least the minimum provisions in the Data Protection Act.

Where cloud services are provided on a bespoke basis, they may be the subject of contractual negotiations between the Data Controller and Data Processor. In such instances a contract can be drawn up that unequivocally meets the requirements of the Act.

However, in many cases – even for quite large business deals – the contract for cloud services is set out in non-negotiable terms and conditions, or with very little scope for variation. If the cloud provider doesn't offer terms and conditions that meet the Act's requirements, there is little that can be done to get them added in.

Ideally, a Data Processor contract should also provide indemnity for the Data Controller against any costs resulting from the Data Processor's failure to deliver. This isn't a legal requirement, but makes sound commercial sense. The standard terms and conditions for cloud services almost inevitably exclude any indemnity for a failure of the service, of course.

This does not mean, however, that the Data Controller should accept the Data Processor's terms uncritically. They should be examined carefully to ensure that no unacceptable risks are being taken. If there are gaps, it may be necessary to consider additional measures that should be taken on the customer side to compensate for any deficiencies in the terms and conditions on offer from the supplier.

One particular concern should be the likelihood that the cloud provider will subcontract delivery of parts of its service. The customer must be able to rely on the whole chain providing the necessary quality of service. Some of these links may be outside the UK or, more pertinently, outside the European Economic Area, which brings additional data protection considerations.

The following provides a quick checklist for issues that a Data Processor contract (or terms and conditions) with a cloud provider should, ideally, address if the application makes, or could make, any use of personal data. Please note that the list is not intended to be a complete or accurate description of the provisions that should be in a contract between a Data Controller and a cloud-based Data Processor, and some of the points may not be relevant in every case.

1) Is it clear that the customer is a Data Controller and the cloud provider is a Data Processor?
2) Is it clear what processing the cloud provider is expected, or entitled, to carry out on the Data Controller's data?
3) Is it explicit that all the customer's data supplied is confidential (unless it is legitimately in the public domain), and that the cloud provider is not to misuse the data or disclose it without the Data Controller's consent, or retain it after the contract ends or the Data Controller stops using the service?
4) Does the cloud provider have effective security (including technical measures, and measures to underwrite the probity of staff), and can the Data Controller audit this effectively?
7) Is there a requirement for the cloud provider to inform the Data Controller immediately of any security breach they become aware of (whether they caused it or not)?
8) Does the cloud provider indemnify the Data Controller for any costs incurred in putting right breaches of data protection brought about deliberately or negligently by

the cloud provider (ideally including costs of reassuring affecting individuals, even if this is not legally required)?

9) Is the cloud provider required not to do anything that would put the Data Controller in breach of the Data Protection Act 1998?

10) Is the cloud provider required to promptly forward to the Data Controller all subject access requests and complaints about any of the processing that they may receive in error?

11) Is the cloud provider required not to process the data, or allow it to be processed, outside the European Economic Area (alternatively not to do so without the Data Controller's prior consent)?

12) Is the cloud provider required not to subcontract any processing (alternatively not to do so without the Data Controller's prior consent)?

CHAPTER 3: SECURITY (SEVENTH DATA PROTECTION PRINCIPLE)

Security is one of the most important safeguards in preventing harm to individuals. The seventh principle says that you must take steps to prevent:

- Unauthorised access
- Accidental loss or damage.

These steps must be 'technical and organisational', and they must be 'appropriate' in terms of the technical options available, and also in terms of the harm that would result in the event of unauthorised access, or loss, or damage.

'Organisational' security measures should always include attention to human factors. In any security breach, at least part of the chain of causation is likely to be an individual taking, or failing to take, appropriate action. The Data Protection liability, however, rests with the organisation. Many of the Information Commissioner's penalty notices highlight failures on the part of the organisation to provide sufficient guidance and training to the individual(s) who were the immediate or partial cause of the breach.

Confidentiality, integrity and availability

The requirements in the seventh principle to prevent unauthorised access, accidental loss or damage, closely mirror the three standard aims of information security: confidentiality, integrity and availability.

Confidentiality is concerned with setting limits on who may have access to specified information, based on their **need to know**. A key feature of confidentiality in UK law is that it applies to information 'given in confidence'. The individual(s) who are given access to the information must be left in no doubt that it is confidential. Any breach of confidentiality in respect of personal data is likely to be 'unauthorised access' which the seventh principle aims to prevent.

In maintaining confidentiality, it is unwise to rely on the probity, conscientiousness or common sense of all those who may handle or have access to data, even if they know the confidentiality boundaries. Technical security measures to prevent unauthorised access should therefore be concerned not merely to prevent deliberate external intrusion. They should also aim to limit access by authorised users to just that information they 'need to know'. Segmentation of data supported by a robust system of access credentials is one of the key controls in this respect.

Data integrity implies that once data has been entered into the system, it should not be modified in an unintended or unauthorised way. This is related to the seventh Principle's requirement to prevent damage.

Availability relates to accidental loss. The concept, however, goes beyond the permanent non-availability that would result from loss of data, to include the requirement for the information to be available whenever it is needed.

Data in transit and at rest

Data 'in transit' is always more vulnerable than data 'at rest'. It is inherent in cloud computing that data will spend more time in transit than it would if it were being processed on an in-house system. Processing personal data in the cloud therefore automatically exposes it to greater risks than it would face behind securely-run perimeter defences of an on-site installation.

That is not to say that the data faces no risks if held on site. It would still be vulnerable to misuse by authorised users, to loss or damage if the backup regime is inadequate, or to external intrusion. In some respects the cloud provider may actually offer greater protection against a backup failure or a poorly-implemented firewall.

However, a survey by BT in July 2014 found that a quarter of respondents that were using cloud services had suffered a data breach where the fault lay with the cloud provider.

There are also regular reports of large amounts of personal data being stolen from online locations. Websites are likely to be particularly vulnerable because, by their very nature, they are designed to have at least an element of public exposure. A website is often the gateway to a large online database of site users, and an integral part of an organisation's relationship with its customers or service users.

Cloud applications that are not intended to be publicly accessible avoid one obvious avenue for compromise but are not immune from security risks. Intrusion is still a possibility. Technical problems could also cause a loss of integrity if the interruption occurs while data is in transit, and any loss or corruption of data is not detected and rectified.

Security in the cloud

Security has to run right the way through, from the device through which the user accesses the application, to the depths of the cloud provider's system, and responsibility for security, end to end, lies with the Data Controller. Normally, as discussed above, the Data Controller is the customer, with the cloud provider acting as a Data Processor.

It is emphatically not enough for the Data Controller to make assumptions about the security measures that may, or may not, be taken by the cloud provider. One clear example of this is the case of the British Pregnancy Advisory Service (BPAS). In February 2014, BPAS was fined[3] £200,000 by the Information Commissioner after its website was hacked into. Highly confidential messages from about 9,700 people, sent via the website to BPAS were stolen, a task made relatively easy by basic security weaknesses on the website. This exploit was intended to undermine BPAS, but could also have placed many of the individuals at considerable personal risk if, as was threatened, the messages had been made public by the hacker. In imposing the penalty, the Information Commissioner made it clear that it was the responsibility of BPAS to instruct the

---

[3] This is a civil monetary penalty. The maximum that can be levied is £500,000 and the penalty can be appealed at tribunal.

web designers and web hosts to implement adequate security, and check that they did so, not just to rely on the assumption that it would be done.

The full monetary penalty notice can be found on the enforcement pages of the Information Commissioner's website.

Additional risks from 'Bring Your Own Device' – or 'Bring Your Own Application'

One of the clear benefits of cloud computing is the possibility of easy (and cheap) access from wherever there is an internet connection. This is often an ideal solution for mobile workers, remote offices and home working. However, users may find reasons for wanting to gain access from personal devices rather than company ones, and the number of devices capable of gaining access has increased rapidly. Desktop computers, laptops, tablets and smartphones all bring their own risks.

This is not the place to give a full description of the issues that need to be addressed in a Bring Your Own Device (BYOD) policy, but those particularly relevant to cloud computing include:

- Controlling access to the device
- Users other than the owner
- Vulnerabilities introduced by other applications on the device
- Opportunities to download data onto the device
- Action to be taken in the event that the device is compromised
- Use of insecure cloud applications to transfer data to or from the device.

Action that can be taken to mitigate each of these risks is discussed in the following chapter.

Even where the Data Controller officially makes no use of cloud applications, a BYOD policy must address the issue of whether the device owner is permitted to use personal cloud-based accounts to transfer data to and from the device, or to work on material that is held on the device. Personal accounts, especially if they can be signed up to at no charge, may well not provide the same levels of security or service availability that business-oriented and paid-for accounts offer. Surveys regularly suggest that this type of 'shadow' cloud use is widespread. Where the Data Controller has corporate accounts with more secure applications, these should be used in preference.

The experience of Aberdeen City Council is instructive. A social worker was permitted to work from home. She had attended a case conference and was typing up the report on her home computer. Apparently she was unaware that the folder in which she stored the document on her computer was set up to synchronise automatically with a cloud-based location. A colleague who had attended the same case conference happened to search for his name on the Web, only to find that the document appeared. There was no security in place to prevent anyone accessing this highly confidential material. The council received a monetary penalty of £100,000, even though neither the computer nor the cloud service was directly under their control. When their employee was authorised to work on confidential material at home, the council should have ensured that appropriate security was in place.

CHAPTER 4: MITIGATING SECURITY RISKS IN THE CLOUD

Mitigating security risks requires a range of measures to be used in combination, in order to provide the end-to-end security discussed above. This publication is not intended to give a detailed description of the technical measures available, and readers with more technical expertise may well be aware of other measures that are appropriate in their particular situation.

Security – like other aspects of data protection – is not something that should be added on as an afterthought. Security should be built into an organisation's infrastructure and become part of how the organisation does business in every respect. Moving to the cloud does not solve the problem if an organisation's existing security architecture and infrastructure is not up to standard; it just adds another element that must be addressed.

Most cloud providers are acutely aware that security has to be a high priority, both for them and their customers. They typically stress the degree to which they take security seriously, and it is often claimed that their security is likely to be considerably better than in most small organisations and some larger ones. This is quite possibly true, but cloud providers may also be a more tempting target, and breaches leading to unauthorised access, as we have seen, undoubtedly do occur.

Cloud security must cover all the elements of the seventh data protection principle, not just preventing unauthorised access but also preventing accidental loss of, or damage to, personal data. Many cloud providers offer indications of the level of service they aim to provide – and may historically have provided – but few are likely to offer unequivocal guarantees. The risk of service non-availability, its potential consequences, and the options for mitigating any damage, must therefore be assessed.

Given that most cloud providers are likely to be Data Processors, the requirement of Schedule 1, Part II, Paragraph 11 of the Data Protection Act must be taken into account. This states that:

Where processing of personal data is carried out by a data processor on behalf of a data controller, the data controller must, in order to comply with the seventh principle –

> *(a) choose a data processor providing sufficient guarantees in respect of the technical and organisational security measures governing the processing to be carried out, and*

> *(b) take reasonable steps to ensure compliance with those measures.*

While physical inspection of a cloud provider's security measures is unlikely to be practical, all reasonable steps must be taken to verify that the provider's security measures up. This should be done by someone with an appropriate level of technical expertise, who is able to ask the right questions and understand the implications of the answers. Without that, it is much more likely that a Data Controller would be penalised should a breach occur.

Areas to assess include checking how access rights are authorised and how users are authenticated, background checks and segregation of duties for the cloud provider's personnel, physical access monitoring and segregation of data.

While the security offered by providers is of course crucial, security of cloud-based systems must start at the customer or Data Controller end, and there is a range of support and advice available at different technical levels. Having got its own house in order, the Data Controller should then carry out due diligence on the security provisions made by the cloud provider.

It is worth pointing out that, in the cloud, security must be managed differently. On an internal server it may be possible to rely heavily on perimeter defences. However, many security products cannot be deployed in a shared environment, and other organisations may be using less secure applications that are within the perimeter of the cloud provider and endanger valuable data. Application-level and 'instance' security should therefore be considered. This could include: firewall or antivirus software that operates within each instance; ensuring that system services are run only where necessary; intrusion detection/prevention systems; and integrity checking or change monitoring software.

Where data is stored partly in the cloud and partly in-house, proper classification of data is vitally important to determine what can safely be stored where, in accordance with legislation, standards, security concerns and the value of the asset.

Cyber Essentials

In June 2014 the UK Government introduced its Cyber Essentials[4] scheme. This sets out the basic controls that all organisations of any size should implement to counter the most common
internet-based security threats. It concentrates on five key areas:

- Firewalls & gateways
- Secure configuration
- Access control
- Malware protection
- Patch management

Many organisations will, of course, have already identified these as being necessary and taken steps to address them. None of them are new or surprising issues, so there is no real excuse for failing to implement appropriate measures. What the Cyber Essentials scheme does offer is a means of proving that the necessary steps have been taken, through external assessment.

---

[4] Information on this was available, at the time of writing, at *www.cyberstreetwise.com/cyberessentials/*

The scheme is intended to be affordable, even for small organisations. There are two levels of assessment. The basic certificate involves completion of a questionnaire which is externally reviewed before the certificate is awarded. The more advanced Cyber Essentials Plus is based on more costly external testing. In each case the certificate – which must be renewed annually – entitles the organisation to display a logo.

Access controls

It is worth bearing in mind that the seventh data protection principle requires security measures to be *technical* and *organisational*. While most of the basic controls in Cyber Essentials are at the technical end, access control clearly has a large organisational component.

Access controls must apply both to the systems that allow users to access cloud applications and to the cloud applications themselves. The seventh data protection principle requires protection against *unauthorised* access. There are many ways of authorising access, but the allocation of logon credentials that then determine the information the user can view or manipulate, has to be a key element. Access privileges should be carefully thought out, so that users see no more information than they need to, and do not have access to functions that are not relevant to them.

This is especially true in the cloud, where the user's location may be less well controlled. It is often worth considering additional precautions – if these are available – such as two-factor authentication, rigorous processes that require good authentication for password recovery or modification, restrictions on the IP addresses from which the application may be accessed, and/or restrictions on the times of day at which any given user is permitted to log-in.

Good segmentation of the data in the cloud system, so that users are restricted in what they can view or modify – and especially what they can download, print or export – also helps to reduce risks. Access to administrative functions must, of course, receive particular attention, and live monitoring of activity in order to flag up unusual behaviour before it is too late, should also be considered. (The key security weakness in the BPAS case described above was a failure to replace the default administrator password.)

Controlling access via personal devices, through a BYOD policy, is particularly important if there is any possibility that confidential personal data may be taken from the cloud and stored on the device. This could be, for example, in the form of emails or information in attachments. Spreadsheets used as informal small databases are a particular hazard. Strict access controls to the device are also essential if the cloud application requires a logon which can be 'remembered' by the device. A BYOD policy should prohibit access to such cloud services by any personal devices that are not secured by the most appropriate access controls available. The Data Controller should also reserve the right to verify the presence of access controls at reasonable opportunities.

This is not just a hypothetical risk. A survey[5] in June 2014 found that 75% of consumers that use social media on mobile devices are automatically logged into their accounts, and even 23% of mobile banking users are automatically logged in. These risks may be acceptable for individuals to choose to take with their own data, but the figures emphasise that employers cannot assume that individuals have taken an appropriate approach to the security of personal devices on which corporate data may be held or accessed.

It is quite likely that personal devices may occasionally, or regularly, be used by others with the permission of the owner. In this case it is essential that these additional users are unable to access any data derived from, or held by, cloud applications. Ideally the device should provide for individual logons and allow only authorised users to access confidential data and associated applications. Again, reservation of the right to verify that these conditions are met may be a reasonable condition of permitting access from the device to corporate cloud data.

---

[5] Commissioned by the software company Intercede.

Other guidance and recommendations

There are, of course, many sources of security guidance. Two that are pitched at a more detailed technical level than Cyber Essentials are from the Information Commissioner and the Open Web Application Security Project (OWASP).

The Information Commissioner produced a report in May 2014 – *Protecting personal data in online services: learning from the mistakes of others*[6]. The report analyses the root causes of security breaches in online systems that have been investigated by the ICO. It identifies eight common vulnerabilities that should, as a matter of course, be addressed. The issues it covers are:

- Software updates
- SQL injection
- Unnecessary services
- Decommissioning of software or services
- Password storage
- Configuration of SSL and TLS
- Inappropriate locations for processing data
- Default credentials.

The OWASP Top Ten is an analysis, updated every three years, of the current most important vulnerabilities in web-based systems and the measures that should be taken to prevent them. The 2013 Top Ten covers:

- Injection
- Broken Authentication and Session Management
- Cross-Site Scripting (XSS)
- Insecure Direct Object References

---

[6] This can be difficult to locate on the Information Commissioner's website. At the time of writing it could be found via a news release dated 12 May 2014 at: *https://ico.org.uk/media/for-organisations/documents/1042221/protecting-personal-data-in-online-services-learning-from-the-mistakes-of-others.pdf*

- Security Misconfiguration
- Sensitive Data Exposure
- Missing Function Level Access Control
- Cross-Site Request Forgery (CSRF)
- Using Components with Known Vulnerabilities
- Unvalidated Redirects and Forwards.

There is clear overlap between this list and the Information Commissioner's, and many of the points are also relevant to the Cyber Essentials controls. It is worth taking a broad view, rather than relying on just one source to identify the security areas that should be given attention.

Regular independent vulnerability assessments and intrusion testing to ensure that applications are protected – from well-documented threats as a minimum – is worth considering.

ISO27001: Information security management

The key international standard on information security is the ISO27000 series, available in the UK from the British Standards Institute.

ISO27001 is the overall framework for information security management, and can be externally certified. It sets out a number of controls that should be in place. Many are directly relevant to cloud computing, including for example:

- System acquisition, development and maintenance (control A.14)
- Access control (control A.9)
- Information transfer (control A.13.2)
- Information security in supplier relationships (control A.15.1)
- Privacy and protection of personally identifiable information (control A.18.1.4)

ISO27001 accreditation is available both to the Data Controller and any cloud suppliers it uses. Many suppliers claim to be ISO27001 compliant, but it is important to check a number of points:

- Has the cloud provider been externally certified, or just self-assessed as compliant?
- Are the credentials of the certifying company satisfactory?
- Does the ISO27001 certificate apply to the issues that concern the data that is intended to be placed in the cloud application, as set out in the supplier's ISO27001 Statement of Applicability?

Data 'in transit'

Data is almost inevitably more at risk when it is 'in transit' rather than 'at rest', which is why information transfer merits a specific control in ISO27001. Many of the Information Commissioner's monetary penalties have involved data going astray in transit (in a range of situations, not always in the context of cloud computing).

When considering a cloud provider's security claims, it is important to check whether these apply equally to data at rest (i.e. while stored on the provider's servers) and data in transit, both between the customer and the cloud provider, and between the cloud provider and any subcontractors that may provide part of the service.

HMG Security Framework

Government agencies, or organisations that have close dealings with government, may also want to review the cloud provider's offering against the HMG Security Framework[7], as well as taking into account the 'cloud first' policy.

The security framework mandates clear accountability for the management of risk, and specifically in relation to information:

- "Staff who are well trained to exercise good judgement, take responsibility and be accountable for the information they handle, including all partner information.
- "Mechanisms and processes to ensure assets are properly classified and appropriately protected.
- "Confidence that security controls are effective and that systems and services can protect the information they carry. There will be an overarching programme of information assurance driven by the Board."

In August 2014, CESG (the National Technical Authority for Information Assurance) published draft guidance on cloud security risk management, listing 14 cloud security principles and setting out in some detail how they should be implemented.

These are:
- Principle 1: Data in transit protection
- Principle 2: Asset protection and resilience
- Principle 3: Separation between consumers
- Principle 4: Governance framework
- Principle 5: Operational security
- Principle 6: Personnel security
- Principle 7: Secure development
- Principle 8: Supply chain security
- Principle 9: Secure consumer management
- Principle 10: Identity and authentication

---

[7] This, and the CESG guidance, are available – unrestricted – on the main government website (.gov.uk).

- Principle 11: External interface protection
- Principle 12: Secure service administration
- Principle 13: Audit information provision to consumers
- Principle 14: Secure use of the service by the consumer

Many of these principles will by now look familiar, as they appear in other schemes we have already referred to. In addition, the CESG guidance gives a useful summary of common approaches to implementing cloud security principles. These are not mutually exclusive and can – indeed often should – be used in combination. They are:

- **Service provider assertion:** The service provider describes how their service complies with the implementation objectives, but is unwilling (or unable) to provide independent validation of compliance.
- **Contractual commitment:** The service provider contractually commits to meet the implementation objectives.
- **Independent validation of assertions:** An independent third party reviews and confirms the service provider's assertions. Service provider [should hold] certificate of compliance with a recognised standard. Certification and implementation of controls [should be] reviewed by a qualified individual.
- **Independent testing of implementation:** Independent testers demonstrate that controls are correctly implemented and objectives are met in practice. A suitably qualified individual [should review] the scope of testing.
- **Assurance in the service design:** A qualified security architect is involved in the design or review of the service architecture.

- **Assurance in the service components:** Independent assurance in the components of a service (such as the products, services, and individuals which a service uses).

In the government G-Cloud programme "cloud security principles [are] a fundamental part of G-Cloud security assurance to help buyers make pragmatic decisions based on relevant, transparent and available information", according to a September 2014 announcement. Suppliers have to provide information about how their products' security maps to the revised government security classification scheme.

COBIT®

COBIT is another framework for information technology management and governance. It is seen as a way to fulfil the requirements of regulatory regimes (such as the US Sarbanes-Oxley Act) for risk mitigation, monitoring and control. COBIT 5 was released in June 2012. It is published by ISACA (originally the Information Systems Audit and Control Association) and its components include:

- Framework, linking IT to business requirements
- Organisation-wide process descriptions that map to responsibility for different aspects of the process
- High-level control objectives
- Management guidelines that include measuring performance
- Maturity models to assess systems and address gaps.

ISAE3402 and SSAE16 (previously SAS70)

Many US organisations mention compliance with SSAE16 which replaced SAS70 (Statement on Auditing Standards: 70) in 2011. SSAE16 (Statement on Standards for Attestation Engagements (SSAE) No. 16, Reporting on Controls at a Service Organization) is intended to provide a US standard that is compatible with the International Service Organisation Reporting Standard ISAE3402.

These are not security standards but are part of an auditing process for financial information. They do, however, examine risk management and clients can ask for additional issues, such as Data Protection Act compliance, to be taken into account.

The statement implies that the service organisation has been audited by an independent auditor and this audit may have examined issues relevant to Data Protection Act compliance.

Additional BYOD considerations

The Data Controller will not usually be able to control which other applications are installed on the device. There is therefore a risk that malicious or ill-behaved applications could introduce security vulnerabilities. Strict data and application segregation can mitigate these risks.

If data can be downloaded from the cloud to the device this is vulnerable to access by other users – with or without permission. Unwise behaviour by the device owner could result, for example, in the device being disposed of while still containing recoverable confidential information. It is also less likely that information that is updated on the device will be reliably backed up.

It is commonplace for devices – especially smartphones that are particularly vulnerable to loss or theft – to allow remote locking and wiping of all data. A device owner may be reluctant to provide the Data Controller with the codes necessary to carry out these operations, or to inform the Data Controller as soon as the device's whereabouts are unknown. This is especially true if data is not segregated, so that the owner's personal information would be wiped at the same time. This would argue for the use of company-issue phones wherever possible. An alternative is to require the device to use an application that ring-fences data acquired from the company's systems, preventing it from being stored on the device, exported from it, or interfered with by other applications on the device.

Again, human factors must be taken into account. For example, a user who finds it onerous to enter a PIN or other security requirement each time they access the device, may be inclined to disengage the access controls after they have been authorised to use the device for accessing their employer's data.

CHAPTER 5: TRANSFERS ABROAD (EIGHTH DATA PROTECTION PRINCIPLE)

If personal data is transferred outside certain European countries, the provisions of the eighth Principle come into play. Storing data on a cloud provider's system abroad counts as a transfer, even if the data is not intended to be used anywhere outside the UK.

As discussed above, it is quite common for a cloud application to be provided by a chain of subcontractors. It is necessary to examine the entire chain in order to assess whether the eighth Principle is engaged.

The eighth Principle aims to achieve an equivalent level of protection for data transferred abroad to that it would receive within the UK.

This level of protection is automatically provided if the jurisdiction to which the data is transferred is within the European Economic Area, because each of those countries has legislation based on the same European Directive (95/46/EC). The European Economic Area comprises the European Union plus Iceland, Liechtenstein and Norway.

Beyond that, a slowly-increasing number of territories have legislation that has been assessed by the European Commission as providing an acceptable level of protection and, as a special case, the US has negotiated the 'Safe Harbor' scheme – discussed in detail below.

This means that, at the time of writing, transfers to anywhere in the table below are treated no differently from a data protection perspective than a transfer within the UK.

Jurisdictions where the requirements of the eighth data protection principle are automatically met (as of October 2014) are shown below:

European Union	Austria, Belgium, Bulgaria, Croatia, Cyprus, Czech Republic, Denmark, Estonia, Finland, France, Germany, Greece, Hungary, Ireland, Italy, Latvia, Lithuania, Luxembourg, Malta, Netherlands, Poland, Portugal, Romania, Slovenia, Slovakia, Spain, Sweden, UK
EEA, outside EU	Iceland, Liechtenstein, Norway
Approved by EC	Andorra, Argentina, Canada, Faroe Islands, Guernsey, Isle of Man, Israel, Jersey, New Zealand, Switzerland, Uruguay
Special case	US, but only where the Safe Harbor scheme applies

Transfers to almost all of Europe are therefore automatically compliant with the eighth Principle, one way or another, but very few others. A few countries, including Australia, Hong Kong and Singapore, for example, have their own data protection laws but these have not been approved by the EC. Transfers outside the locations in the table above are only permitted if they meet one of the exemptions set out in Schedule 4 of the Act. These include:

- Consent of the Data Subject.
- Necessity in connection with a contract (or prospective contract) between the Data Subject and the Data Controller or a contract with another party at the request of the Data Subject or in their interests.
- Necessity for reasons of substantial public interest.
- Terms "of a kind approved by the Commissioner as ensuring adequate safeguards for the rights and freedoms of data subjects".
- When "authorised by the Commissioner as being made in such a manner as to ensure adequate safeguards for the rights and freedoms of data subjects".

"Adequate safeguards" can be provided through the use of one of the four sets of model contract clauses that have been approved by the EC[8]. Two of these are designed for use when a Data Controller is transferring data to a Data Processor (one of which is no longer acceptable for new contracts). However, most cloud services are not offered on terms that incorporate the EC model clauses.

Intra-company transfers can be protected through binding corporate rules (BCRs) that have been approved by the Information Commissioner. These would not, of course, be relevant to cloud computing where the recipient overseas is a Data Processor, but they could apply where a company has a private cloud located wholly or partially overseas.

Other contractual arrangements may also suffice to provide adequate safeguards, and in the case of cloud services based on standard terms and conditions, this may be one of the few options available. The onus, as ever, is on the Data Controller to demonstrate that appropriate steps have been taken and that the terms and conditions do provide adequate safeguards.

If you are relying on Data Subject consent you must make your Data Subjects fully aware that you intend to transfer their data abroad, so that they can make their own decision on whether the risk is acceptable. In most cloud computing situations consent is unlikely to be a practicable option.

Necessity in relation to the performance of a contract is unlikely to be an acceptable claim in respect of cloud computing, because it can always be argued that equivalent cloud services could have been obtained from providers within the EEA.

Safe Harbor

Some commentators would seriously question whether the Safe Harbor scheme in the US provides an adequate basis for data protection compliance when using cloud services. The scheme

---

[8] Explained in detail on the Information Commissioner's website.

was designed to provide a basis for transferring data between the US and Europe that did not require the US government to put a data protection regime in place. Among its claimed drawbacks are:

- It is largely self-assessed and self-policed; it has no statutory backing.
- The mechanisms for redress can be cumbersome and expensive.
- It only covers data types that are subject to Federal Trade Commission or Department of Transportation oversight. HR data, for example, is not covered.
- Most entries in the Safe Harbor register[9] – with a few notable exceptions – refer to data that the US company holds about individuals abroad who are direct customers, but do not refer explicitly to any personal data held on behalf of customer organisations as part of a cloud service or to the cloud provider's role as a Data Processor.
- Some investigations have uncovered companies claiming to be signed up to Safe Harbor when, in fact, they are not, while other complaints suggest that US companies make use of personal data in ways that are not covered by their Safe Harbor statements. In 2014 the then European Union justice minister said that the Safe Harbor agreement "may not be so safe after all" and would be reviewed.

Despite this, the agreement is accepted by the EU as providing an acceptable level of protection, and few people worry about the finer points. If a cloud provider based in the US is signed up to Safe Harbor, therefore, the risk of being found in breach of the eighth data protection principle appears to be very small.

Some government data, however, is required to be held within the EEA, or even just within the UK, and some Data Controllers prefer not to rely on Safe Harbor. In these cases, a

---

[9] The register can be consulted at
https://safeharbor.export.gov/list.aspx

cloud service where the data is guaranteed to be held only within Europe would be preferable.

Until recently this was easier said than done. Many of the big providers either refused to say where their data was held (for 'security' reasons), or explicitly stated that it would be held in the US. Now, though, many have accepted that there is a commercial advantage in providing at least the option for data to be held only within the EEA, and it is rare to find a service that holds all its data in the US, come what may.

It is also worth pointing out that data comes under the protection of the EU Data Protection regime as soon as it is held within Europe, even if it originates outside Europe, relates to Data Subjects outside Europe, and is essentially used only outside Europe.

CHAPTER 6: OTHER DATA PROTECTION PRINCIPLES

Although the seventh and eighth data protection principles are those with the greatest relevance to cloud computing, it is worth looking briefly at the other six.

First Data Protection Principle (Fairness, Transparency and Choice)

This principle, as well as making a general requirement of fairness, specifies that Data Subjects must have ready access to information about who is using their data and what for – the Transparency requirement – and that they must, in some cases, give consent for this.

There is also a requirement to indicate who – either in general or specifically – the data may be disclosed to or shared with. Transferring data to a cloud provider does not count as a disclosure, since the Data Controller takes full responsibility for restricting what the Data Processor may do with the data and for security. There is therefore no obligation to inform the Data Subject when a Data Processor is used.

The situation is different, however, in cases where the cloud provider is a Data Controller in their own right. This might occur, for example, where the cloud provider is dealing directly with the Data Subject through an ancillary activity – such as the situation with a payment processor described on page 10. In some cases the cloud provider may even reserve the right to use data about their customer's Data Subjects for the cloud provider's own purposes. In both these cases the Data Subject must be informed that their data will be shared with the secondary Data Controller.

In addition to providing information, the Data Controller must consider whether Data Subjects should be given a choice over the use of their data. In many cases choice is not appropriate, because of the sixth Schedule 2 Condition, 'legitimate interests' (see page 6). Where a choice is offered, it should be a genuine choice; there is rarely much benefit in placing mandatory consent – for example for a transfer abroad – deep in the terms and conditions to which a Data Subject has to agree. It is far better to provide the information clearly and indicate that the transfer will take place if the Data Subject goes ahead with whatever transaction is being provided.

Second Data Protection Principle (Specified and limited purposes)

This Principle has no specific implications for cloud computing.

Third Data Protection Principle (Adequate, Relevant and not Excessive)

The main concern with this Principle would be if a cloud application is designed in such a way that it requires the collection of more data than is required for the purpose, or does not permit the collection of sufficient data.

Where the Data Controller has complete control over the design of the application this should not arise, but there may be cases where, for cost reasons, an off-the-shelf application is preferred. It would not be acceptable from a data protection point of view to make use of a cloud application that was not flexible enough to match the data collected to the purpose of the application.

Fourth Data Protection Principle (Accuracy)

Again, the main concern with this Principle is likely to be the flexibility of the application. To take a simple and perhaps rare example, if an application were designed, or set up, to use only the American format for short dates (MM/DD/YY) instead of the European format (DD/MM/YY) it would be more than likely that a significant proportion of users from the UK would enter dates incorrectly.

Fifth Data Protection Principle (Limited retention)

It is increasingly difficult to ensure that data is erased entirely once there is no longer any necessity to retain it. Backup and archive copies may well exist, even when the live version of the data is deleted – especially when a cloud provider takes responsibility for backing up, and may also keep data at multiple locations to improve resilience. One of the drawbacks of cloud computing is that the Data Controller may often be unaware of where the data is physically held, or by whom. It is, nevertheless, the Data Controller's responsibility to ensure that data is not retained longer than necessary, in relation to the purpose for which it is held.

Concerns about the proliferation and persistence of personal data are growing. The European Court of Justice (ECJ) ruling in May 2014 on what is erroneously referred to as the 'right to be forgotten', is just one indication of this development.

It is worth clarifying that the ECJ ruling did not create a right to be forgotten. It required Google to remove its *links* to data that was inaccurate, inadequate, irrelevant or excessive for the purposes for which *Google itself* was processing the data. (The third and fourth data protection principles can be clearly recognised in that list.) The information being linked to could remain on the public record where it had always been.

The proposed new European Regulation (see below) includes a version of the 'right to be forgotten' – the final extent of which remains to be seen. However, the immediate impact on most Data Controllers will be minimal. The only really surprising thing about the ECJ ruling is how emphatically it brings search engines within the rules of data protection. The rest of the decision was based firmly on Principles that had already been in force for nearly 15 years.

Sixth Data Protection Principle (Data Subject rights)

The key Data Subject rights protected by the sixth principle are:

- The right to prevent their data being used for direct marketing of any kind.
- The right of Subject Access.
- The right, in certain cases, to prevent processing likely to cause substantial damage or substantial address to that individual or another.
- The right to have incorrect data corrected and excessive data removed.

It is worth looking briefly at the cloud computing implications of these rights.

When data on the same person is held in more than one place, synchronisation becomes an issue. A 'no marketing' flag in one system may not be implemented across the board. For example, individuals' details may be held on a CRM system which is used for occasional mailings and for recording transactions, while email marketing is carried out through a cloud application. If someone uses the automatic 'unsubscribe' option in an email they may expect to receive no more contact from the organisation, only to find that some marketing is also being sent from the CRM system. Standalone cloud applications therefore pose the same issues as standalone systems on site, but the options for integration between systems may be limited, and may have to be carried out manually.

Data held in multiple systems also makes responding properly to a Subject Access Request more onerous. Unless the Data Subject explicitly limits their request, the Data Controller is obliged to provide a copy of all the data held on that individual (apart from any that may legitimately be redacted to protect third parties), regardless of where it is held.

Cloud computing is less likely to cause distinct problems with the remaining two Data Subject rights in the list.

CHAPTER 7: OTHER LEGAL AND TECHNICAL IMPLICATIONS FOR CLOUD CONTRACTS

The requirements for a contract between a Data Controller and a Data Processor have been discussed on page 13, while the contractual implications when cloud processors are based outside the EEA are discussed on page 36 onwards.

This chapter looks briefly at other legal and technical issues with data protection implications.

A major consideration is the requirement in the seventh data protection principle to take appropriate steps against accidental loss or damage to data, and the wider question of the data being available when required. Problems could arise from:

- Loss of service –
  - at the provider's end, if their system goes down.
  - at the customer's end, if the Internet connection is impaired.
- Possible obstacles to a change of provider if the service proves unsatisfactory, caused by the data being held in a proprietary format.
- Possible difficulty retrieving the data if the service ceases, or in case of a dispute with the provider.
- Difficulty in making a usable and comprehensive backup of the data independently from the provider's system, as additional security in case of problems.

It is rare for cloud providers to offer guaranteed levels of service, and failures do happen from time to time. These risks cannot be ignored, and contingency plans should be in place.

Retrieving data in the event of a breakdown in the commercial relationship may be less easy to provide for, which is why a readily usable backup, independent of the cloud provider's systems, is likely to be essential. Not only may the format in which data is stored make retrieval of useful data awkward, there is also the question of precisely where it is stored and how to access it.

Few cloud providers control all the assets involved in providing their service. Frequently, there are several links in the chain: the service provider may be a reseller of another company's product; the data storage may be subcontracted out, and the subcontractor may not own the physical hardware on which the data is stored. Should any of these links break, there is no direct contract between the Data Controller and the ultimate holder of the data. To complicate matters further, the different companies in the chain may be based in different legal jurisdictions.

Other points to watch out for in standard terms and conditions include:

- Contract terms which make the supplier a Data Controller in their own right (for example, if they reserve the right to make use of the customer's data, or some of it, for their own purposes).
- Unilateral changes in terms and conditions by the provider.

These concerns all indicate that it is very important to study carefully the legal and technical underpinning of any cloud service before entrusting personal data to it, or basing critical processes on cloud applications. It is not always easy to piece together all the necessary information, and some providers are better than others at making it all readily available in a comprehensible form. A cursory review is not enough, and those entrusted with the review should have the necessary legal or technical expertise to understand the implications of the information they obtain.

The concerns also contribute to an essential requirement in any cloud application: ensuring that there is a reliable way to continue business if the relationship with the cloud provider breaks down in any way. An escrow or recovery procedure should not just be put in place, but should also be tested and documented so that it can be reliably and promptly brought into action if required.

Overriding jurisdictions

Since many cloud applications involve data being processed outside of the UK, this could mean that different laws – sometimes very different laws – could apply to all, or part, of the operation. Again, this is something that must be taken into account as a potential risk, if the supplier claims to be bound by the laws of a different jurisdiction.

Most countries have laws allowing the authorities to access data in what they deem to be the public interest, but the one which is most often talked about is the US Patriot Act. This is ostensibly anti-terrorist, but has also been used in non-terrorist cases. It requires any US-based company to provide any information it holds to the US Government, on demand (even if the data is not in the US). Some suppliers undertake to inform their customers before passing on data, but they may not offer this and – in some cases – may not even be allowed to inform the customer of access.

The revelations in 2013 on the extent to which the Prism programme allowed US (and other) authorities to by-pass legislative restrictions on accessing data on the Internet, merely reinforced these concerns.

Most organisations are probably reasonably sanguine about the fairly remote possibility of their data becoming of interest to the authorities, but the possibility should still be included in any risk assessment.

Responding to breaches

The Information Commissioner provides guidance on data security breach management that sets out a four-stage process:

- Containment and recovery
- Assessment of ongoing risk
- Notification of breach

- Evaluation and response.

In addition to this, most organisations will be concerned at the reputational damage that a serious breach would be likely to bring. It is common practice to have a prepared statement in place that can be adapted to the specific circumstances, and to allocate responsibility for communications with the media and with regulators. It may be worth considering whether arrangements should also be made to involve the cloud provider in the response, if the breach takes place as a result of a failure for which they are partly or wholly responsible.

CHAPTER 8: ENFORCEMENT

The potential costs of a data protection breach are incalculable, although many breaches do not in fact lead to seriously adverse outcomes. The three main risks are:

- A fine (civil monetary penalty) from the Information Commissioner.
- Compensation to affected individuals for damage and associated distress.
- Reputational damage to the Data Controller responsible.

The maximum fine is £500,000 (but see following chapter). The Information Commissioner's strategy is to identify particularly serious breaches and impose sufficiently large penalties as to attract attention and encourage others to take steps to avoid ending up in the same situation. Research carried out for the Commissioner in 2014 found evidence that this approach was having the desired effect.

Examples have been given above of fines imposed for security breaches associated with cloud activities. Although a fine could be imposed for a serious breach of any of the eight data protection principles, in fact almost all have been imposed for breaches of the seventh principle – security. Note that in order to attract a fine, there does not have to be any evidence that actual harm has resulted from the breach. Fines have been imposed in cases where the data has either been recovered before it could be misused, or has disappeared without trace and does not appear to have fallen into the wrong hands.

Another feature to note is that the Information Commissioner's justification for imposing a fine frequently cites the lack of effective policies and procedures, either because they were not specific and detailed enough to address the risks, or because the staff involved were not given sufficient training to be aware of the course of action they were expected to take.

This suggests strongly that all users of cloud-based applications should be given clear guidance and training on how these should be used (or even not used, in the case of personal cloud accounts).

Compensation to individuals is less well reported. Claims must be based on tangible damage.

All enforcement action by the Information Commissioner is published on his website. Action short of a fine can include Enforcement Notices – setting out action to be taken, where failure to comply is a criminal offence – and binding undertakings committing the Data Controller to remedial action. Any of these could, as a result of their publication, lead to reputational damage.

Other costs associated with a breach could include:

- Notifying potentially affected individuals, if this is appropriate.
- Assistance to potentially affected individuals, such as, for example, providing them with credit reference support where there is a danger of ID theft, or other damage to their credit rating.
- Data restoration, where the breach involves loss or damage of important information.

CHAPTER 9: THE PROPOSED NEW EU REGULATION AND OTHER MEASURES

The EU Directive (95/46/EC) on which the Data Protection Act 1998 is based, was first mooted in 1993 and agreed in 1995. The intervening 20 years have seen dramatic technical changes which could not have been foreseen at the time. Cloud computing is one of these.

Many would say that the Directive has actually coped quite well with these changes, as it was couched largely in terms of general principles and could therefore be seen as technologically neutral. Cloud computing and other developments have, however, started to raise issues that the existing data protection regime does not really have answers to. In addition, a review would also allow some modification to be made in the light of experience.

The process began with the publication of a proposed Regulation by the European Commission in late 2011. After a great deal of discussion and negotiation, the European Parliament approved a revised version in October 2013. The next stage is agreement by the Council of Ministers, where national preferences and viewpoints are likely to come into play. The European elections in 2014 brought about significant changes, both in the Parliament and subsequently in the Commission, so that, at the time of writing, it is hard to predict the final form in which the Regulation will emerge.

Once the Regulation is approved, there is a lead-in period, but after that it takes effect immediately. A Regulation is in effect an EU-wide law; it doesn't depend on individual countries bringing in their own legislation. Even in the event of the UK leaving the EU it is unlikely that free trade arrangements would be able to continue without the UK adopting legislation compatible with the Regulation.

Many of the issues addressed in the draft Regulation are not specific to cloud applications. However, it is worth being aware of some possible changes that the new Regulation might bring about. These include:

- **Security:** There are more specific obligations on the security measures to be taken.
- **Data and Data Processors:** There is more clarity on how the responsibility is shared out when two or more organisations work together, either as joint Data Controllers or as Data Controller and Data Processor.
- **Data Protection management:** The rules on how organisations must manage Data Protection are much more specific, including provision for every Data Controller (possibly excluding small ones) to have a suitably qualified Data Protection Officer.
- **Breach notification:** All (or at least many more than at present) data breaches would have to be notified to the Information Commissioner.
- **Penalties:** Far higher maximum penalties for breaches are a possibility, based on the size of the organisation. The proposal is for penalties to be up to 2% of global turnover.
- **Basis of processing:** There are minor changes, such as requiring 'data minimisation'.
- **Erasure:** Data Subjects would have the right, in some circumstances, to require data to be erased. This has been erroneously described as a 'right to be forgotten'.

The EU Commission has also said that it may establish standards for terms and conditions for cloud computing services. Progress towards this appears to have been made with the establishment of the Cloud Select Industry Group, under whose auspices an industry group (largely appearing to comprise US companies) produced draft standard guidelines[10]

---

[10] At the time of writing these can be found at:
http://ec.europa.eu/information_society/newsroom/cf/dae/document.cf m?action=display&doc_id=6138

in June 2014. The guidelines set out a process for ensuring that cloud computing terms and conditions are clear and comparable between providers. They do not, however, appear to redress the balance between the provider and the customer in terms of the negotiability of cloud terms and conditions, or to provide mandatory minimum standards.

The next step is for these guidelines to be tested with cloud users.

CHAPTER 10: CHECKLIST

Throughout this publication various recommendations have been made. They are summarised here for convenience.

☐ Before embarking on a cloud computing development ensure that your organisation's information (and especially IT) security framework is sound, and that responsibility for information security is clearly allocated.

☐ Ensure that your organisation's approach to data protection compliance is well thought out, and that responsibility is clearly allocated.

☐ Before selecting a cloud provider, consider whether your data needs to be retained in the European Economic Area, and if so, make this a key selection criterion.

☐ For all cloud providers under consideration, check the contract (or standard terms and conditions) very carefully, especially for:

- ownership of the data
- security undertakings, and certified security standards
- location of data (UK?, EEA?, etc.), and whether you have any control over this
- any mention of liability the provider accepts or excludes
- any mention of whether the provider uses subcontractors
- arrangements for you to make your own backups, in addition to those made automatically by the provider
- how you obtain access to your data in the case of wanting to change provider

- what happens to your data if the provider (or one of its subcontractors) goes out of business, or if you get into a dispute with the provider
- any provision for the supplier to use your data for its own purposes
- mechanisms by which you can verify, for example, where the data is held.

☐ Verify any claims made by the providers for compliance with, for example:
- ISO27001
- Safe Harbor, in the case of a US-based company.

☐ It is impossible to eliminate all risks. Assess the risks and prepare a risk assessment so that the appropriate people in your organisation can make an informed decision.

☐ Ensure that any contractors assisting in setting up the cloud application are given clear instructions about the security measures they should be implementing.

☐ Once the cloud service is in place, consider commissioning external testing to ensure that it has been configured correctly and is not vulnerable to any of the well-documented security threats.

☐ Ensure that access to the cloud application and the data it holds is adequately controlled, especially if it may be accessed by users working at home, or on their own devices.

☐ Provide adequate training and guidance for all users, so that they know both how to use the system, and how to ensure that personal data placed in it is appropriately handled.

REFERENCES

Cloud Security and Governance: Who's on your Cloud? by Sumner Blount and Rob Zanella

Securing Cloud Services: A pragmatic approach to security architecture in the Cloud by Lee Newcombe

Cloud Computing: Assessing the risks by Jared Carstensen, JP Morgenthal and Bernard Golden

Above the Clouds: Managing Risk in the World of Cloud Computing by Kevin T McDonald

From a legal perspective: *Cloud Computing a practical introduction to the legal issues*, by Renzo Marchini

See also the Cloud Security Alliance or CSA (*www.cloudsecurityalliance.org*) which provides a security framework developed with cloud considerations in mind - the Cloud Controls Matrix (CCM).

ITG RESOURCES

IT Governance Ltd sources, creates and delivers products and services to meet the real-world, evolving IT governance needs of today's organisations, directors, managers and practitioners.

The IT Governance website (*www.itgovernance.co.uk*) is the international one-stop-shop for corporate and IT governance information, advice, guidance, books, tools, training and consultancy. On the website you will find the following pages related to the subject matter of this book:

www.itgovernance.co.uk/data-protection.aspx

www.itgovernance.co.uk/cloud-computing.aspx.

Publishing Services

IT Governance Publishing (ITGP) is the world's leading IT-GRC publishing imprint that is wholly owned by IT Governance Ltd.

With books and tools covering all IT governance, risk and compliance frameworks, we are the publisher of choice for authors and distributors alike, producing unique and practical publications of the highest quality, in the latest formats available, which readers will find invaluable.

www.itgovernancepublishing.co.uk is the website dedicated to ITGP. Other titles published by ITGP that may be of interest include:

- Data Protection Compliance in the UK

  www.itgovernance.co.uk/shop/p-515-data-protection-compliance-in-the-uk.aspx

- Cloud Computing: Assessing the Risks

  www.itgovernance.co.uk/shop/p-465-cloud-computing-assessing-the-risks.aspx

- Securing Cloud Services

www.itgovernance.co.uk/shop/p-1098-securing-cloud-services-a-pragmatic-approach-to-security-architecture-in-the-cloud.aspx.

We also offer a range of off-the-shelf toolkits that give comprehensive, customisable documents to help users create the specific documentation they need to properly implement a management system or standard. Written by experienced practitioners and based on the latest best practice, ITGP toolkits can save months of work for organisations working towards compliance with a given standard.

To see the full range of toolkits available please visit:

www.itgovernance.co.uk/shop/c-129-toolkits.aspx.

Books and tools published by IT Governance Publishing (ITGP) are available from all business booksellers and the following websites:

www.itgovernance.eu   *www.itgovernanceusa.com*

www.itgovernance.in   *www.itgovernancesa.co.za*

www.itgovernance.asia.

Training Services

IT Governance provides a range of data protection training and staff awareness courses to suit your corporate needs.

Our public DPA Foundation Course is a one-day introduction to Data Protection Act (DPA) compliance, and is delivered by a data protection practitioner who is experienced in applying the DPA's principles to real-life situations. This course offers advice about, and a thorough understanding of, the DPA's requirements.

For more information, visit our website: *www.itgovernance.co.uk/shop/p-525-dpa-foundation-course.aspx*.

In-house training courses may be more cost-effective if you have a number of staff who wish to understand the requirements of the DPA. At IT Governance we are experienced providers of customised staff awareness courses.

For more information see: *www.itgovernance.co.uk/shop/p-521-dpa-staff-awareness-e-learning-course.aspx*.

If you are a data protection officer/practitioner yourself, you may want a formal qualification and an advanced level of knowledge to best advise your organisation. IT Governance offers the BCS ISEB in Data Protection, a five-day practical course with a written examination, successful completion of which will demonstrate an advanced level of knowledge and ability.

For more information, visit our website: *www.itgovernance.co.uk/shop/p-422-certificate-in-data-protection-training-course.aspx*.

Professional Services and Consultancy

As a compliance specialist, IT Governance has been helping organisations achieve and maintain DPA compliance for over ten years.

The IT Governance DPA gap analysis service can help you assess your organisation's current level of compliance with the DPA, including the exact standing of your current legal situation, security practices and operating procedures in relation to DPA compliance.

By examining procedures such as direct marketing practices, fair processing notices, and retention and deletion procedures, our expert data protection consultants can identify any gaps, and then create and implement a remedial plan that will not only enable you to bring your business into full compliance with the DPA, but also will ensure that you maintain your compliance in the future.

We will tell you what you need to know quickly and effectively; then, if you need our help to achieve DPA compliance, we can assist with remediation, including ISO27001 and ISO22301 implementation.

For more information, see

www.itgovernance.co.uk/dpa-compliance-consultancy.aspx.

Newsletter

IT governance is one of the hottest topics in business today, not least because it is also the fastest moving.

You can stay up to date with the latest developments across the whole spectrum of IT governance subject matter, including: risk management, information security, ITIL and IT service management, project governance, compliance and so much more, by subscribing to ITG's core publications and topic alert emails.

Simply visit our subscription centre and select your preferences:

www.itgovernance.co.uk/newsletter.aspx.

EU for product safety is Stephen Evans, The Mill Enterprise Hub, Stagreenan, Drogheda, Co. Louth, A92 CD3D, Ireland. (servicecentre@itgovernance.eu)

www.ingramcontent.com/pod-product-compliance
Lightning Source LLC
LaVergne TN
LVHW052311060326
832902LV00021B/3830